CRAZY ICE CREAM

Written and Illustrated by

Finley Finch

Theodore, his little sister, Skylar, and his best friend Samuel eat ice cream at their favorite ice cream parlor, Captain Cone's Super Creamery.

Theodore's favorite flavor is Pickle Onion Raspberry Swirl.

Skylar and Samuel like Cream Cheese Fish Sticks with butterscotch swirls and whipped cream.

Fatima, her little brother, Ayden, and her best friend Chloe eat ice cream at the county fair.

Fatima's favorite flavor is Corn Bread with Navy Bean.

Ayden and Chloe like Tomato with Mustard flavor covered with chunks of okra and eggplant.

Logan and his twin sister, Mariam, eat ice cream when they go ice skating.

Logan's favorite flavor is Spinach Broccoli Pea.

Mariam likes Mochi Jalapeno Salmon flavor.

Weston eats ice cream whenever he visits the city.

His favorite flavor is Garlic Beef Stew with soy sauce and cinnamon.

Whenever he can add fish egg sprinkles, he's extra super happy.

Brielle eats ice cream when she's happy and she's happy when she eats ice cream.

Her favorite flavor is Butternut Squash with Green Olives.

Rock candy is the topping she uses more than any other, but she does like dried banana slices, too.

Kingston eats ice cream at carnivals and festivals.

His favorite flavor is Beet and Blue Cheese with Carrot Chips.

He prefers waffle cones, but that doesn't mean he isn't happy with a sugar cone.

Ruby goes for walks in the evening and eats ice cream along the way.

Her favorite flavor is Baked Bean and Peppercorn with pickled strawberries.

Before she finishes the cone, she shares crumbs with pigeons.

Angel eats ice cream in huge bites.

His favorite flavor is Edamame and Spiced Goat Cheese with spicy thai peanuts.

When he's feeling extra bold and crazy, he uses ghost pepper sauce, too.

Vivian eats ice cream after her workout.

Her favorite flavor is Cilantro Lime Pancake Batter with green curry.

After eating her ice cream, she eats a caramel and cream pop.

Leo eats ice cream cones in a single bite.

Even though he barely tastes it, he still prefers Dijon Mustard
Basil Date flavored ice cream cones.

Leo's ice cream cones take an entire gallon to make.

Olive licks her ice cream cones slowly.

Her first choice is Miso Lavender Mushroom with licorice sauce.

Sometimes she takes too long to finish and gets sunburned.

Ryan goes to the park to eat ice cream while people watching.

His favorite flavor is Balsamic Tabasco Cabbage with a splash of vinegar.

When the weather is nice, Ryan eats two ice creams. One when he arrives, and one before he goes home.

Amelia eats ice cream on the way to her job as a dog walker.

Her favorite flavor is Mayonnaise Matcha Lychee Boba.

She tried sharing once with the poodles she walks, but they didn't like it.

Roman smiles when he eats ice cream cones, and he always eats three or four. Sometimes five.

His favorite flavor is Avocado Egg-Salad Celery with bits of bell pepper.

Once, he ate seven, and got a stomachache.

London eats ice cream after breathing fire.

Her favorite flavor is Teriyaki Lemon Mint with cheddar cheese nacho sauce.

After eating an ice cream, she can't breathe fire for an hour or two.

Henry eats ice cream cones when he walks in the city.

His favorite flavor is Lobster Cranberry Stuffing with squid ink sauce.

He doesn't understand why poodles don't like ice cream. Do you?

Thank you for reading this
Finley Finch
Early Reader and Bedtime Storybook!

CRAZY ICE CREAM

To contact us:
information@adverley.com

Made in the USA
Middletown, DE
07 October 2024

62157141R00020